Essentials of

Data Science

Crash Course for Beginners

By:

Max Anderson

Table of Contents

Introduction

Thank you for purchasing this mini course on the essentials of data science. This mini course provides a super basic looking to data science, what it is, and the three main components that make up data science. Data science is a very mainstream word that gets thrown around a lot, but its actual definition is quite vague. This mini course is designed to help those of you who are curious about data science develop a better and more specific understanding of the topic.

There are definitely more advanced techniques within data science such as machine learning, but even these can be traced back to the three essential components that we'll cover in this book. Before we get straight into it, I thought I'd quickly introduce myself my name is Max and I work as a data scientist. After getting my degree in physics, I find myself more and more drawn into the world of data science. So instead of diving into the realm of physics research, I taught myself all the tools and techniques a data scientist needs. And shortly after landed my dream data science job. I've since also started teaching data science to others and have been fortunate enough to teach what is currently over 9,000 students the skills I have gathered and learned over the past five years of my data science journey. So let's jump right into it.

Chapter one

What is data science?

Well you can define data science in different ways depending on the angle you are approaching it from, but the in the simplest sense, data science is all about transforming data into information. Many people talk about data, big data and all those terminologies, but data by itself isn't really that useful until you can turn it into information. If you just have a bunch of numbers appearing somewhere, and it's just so much that no one can make sense of it, it is so vague, you need a data scientist to be able to transform all of these vagueness and noise that's going on and you need to be able to extract information from it and that's what a data scientist does.

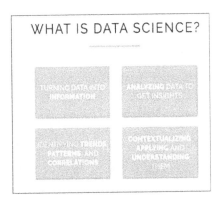

Now what you do with this information or how you get this information is through analysing your data. So a big part of it would be cleaning things up, doing some processes on it and then you analyse once you've clean things up. And that is one of the ways that you can then get information out of your data. Through this analysis, you can continue on and you see trends and patterns and all types of correlations. All of these things again build up into this turning data into information components. And then ultimately, you also need to contextualize everything that you have because your computer can't do that for you. Your computer can crunch the numbers but it's your responsibility also to make sense what's in front of you, and even if you see something, you just don't blindly trust it, but you need to understand some things such as, where am I at, where am I coming from, where is this data coming from? You need to be able to contextualize these things and then of course be able to apply as well as understand them. And once you have this data, it's great, but turning it into an information, into great information that you can use and directly apply, that's where the real power lies. And that's also the role of a data scientist, that's what data science pretty much is.

What Does a Data Scientist Do?

Well, we already talked about this just a little bit, but let's go over it again and give more concrete examples. A data scientist would for example get and process this raw data and then convert it into something a little bit cleaner. So you can imagine you have a data stream coming in, and you have this measuring device and is constantly just measuring all sorts of data. And because nothing is really constant, everything will be fluctuating up and down. A data scientist would take all of this data and clean it up a little bit, maybe reduce this fluctuation that isn't supposed to be there and then put it into a format so that you can easily plot it against some things.

Once this data is cleaner, you can start doing some calculations on them, figuring out the core statistical components; like what is the average values of these? What am I really dealing with? Getting a first look at, a first understanding what it is actually that you're tackling. And then once you have this understanding, then you can start to do some visualizations which helped you as a data scientist, maybe see some trends or patterns already. But visualization is also really key because they help you to show the information to other people and they are great means of communication. So they help both you as a data scientist, as well as helping others when you try to convey this information to them.

And finally, you have to suggest some applications of the information. So it's not really enough to just be able to look at it and say, yeah, I see it goes up and down and that's good, but what does that mean? How does this transfer into something useful? And that's also one of the key roles of a data scientist; transferring information into knowledge! And so you've got this data into information step, but you also need to transfer this information into knowledge. And those are two really powerful things that are worth a lot, and that's pretty much what a data scientist focuses on.

And then you can go further and take this data and do machine learning with it if you really understand what's going on, or if you have some hypotheses of what could happen. So you can take things a lot further. But ultimately turning data into information and then into knowledge, that's your role.

Essentials Components of Data Science

Let's get into the essential techniques or the essential components of data science. The first essential component and we already talked about this is statistics. And basically we're going to cover this later on but, let's just give a quick wrap down.

ESSENTIALS OF DATA SCIENCE
STATISTICS

- Understanding the different types of data you can encounter
- Understanding key statistical terms
  - Types of means
  - Fluctuations in data
- Splitting up, grouping, and segmenting data points

In statistics, you need to understand different data types that you can encounter. Data can come in different ways and we'll go again into more detail with this later. But it's not just about you having a bunch of numbers. Data can come in very many different ways depending on the field that you're in, and so you need to be prepared and you need to be aware that data may not always just be a direct number for you. Then of course, you need to understand some key statistical terms like: the different types of means and also understanding fluctuations in data. And the reason that this is important is because these key statistical terms give you an overview of how this data is behaving, and depending on how the data is behaving you may want to approach it differently.

So if you know that your data is very clean, there's a very little fluctuation, then if you visualize things you can probably trust what's going on, or if you want to maybe fit some curves to it or something. But if you see there's a lot of fluctuation in your data, visualizing it is going to be much more difficult because you just see jumps everywhere, and you're not really sure which of this is actually true, and which of this is caused by some interference somewhere or someone messing with your system. All of these things will be hinted to you through statistical terms. So it's probably good that you're comfortable with these things and that you can be able to get some meaning out of them.

And then finally in statistics you should be able to split up, group, or segment data points. So that when you have this big data set, you want to be able to split it up into smaller things, compare different regions, look more detail into some things and maybe, isolate two components, because these things are probably going to be important. So being able to pinpoint and isolate and meddle with the data a little bit, these are the kind of statistical components that we're going to look into.

Data Visualization

The next big thing and we've already talked about this too is data visualization, and we'll see why data visualization is a really key skill for data scientists. And then we're also going to be covering different types of graphs that you can use and how you can compare different number of variables. So for example, you can have one variable graphs where you only look at one thing and you only want to look at this and you want to see how this changes. You have your typical two variable graphs where you have this X and a Y-axis and then you can see how the two variables relate to each other, or you can have three variable or even higher variable graphs where you plot maybe three different things or even more if you want as long as it makes sense next to each other, so that you can compare multiple things at the same time.

Programming

ESSENTIALS OF DATA SCIENCE

PROGRAMMING

- Why knowing how to program makes your life so much easier
  - Ease of automation
  - Being able to customize, explore, prototype and test
- Essential packages to use in Python
  - Pandas for data analysis
  - Matplotlib and seaborn for data visualization

Now we come to the other big thing that you're probably going to need as a data scientist; which is the ability to program. Now, not every data scientist can do this, but this is really essential in my opinion, to your role as a data scientist. Because knowing how to program is going to make your life so much easier. If you know how to program, you can take your ideas and thoughts and you can put them into actions in the computer and you can just automate everything. You can customize things, you can explore, you can prototype, you can test and you're not reliant on some application. You don't have to master some application and if it doesn't work or if one feature isn't there, you have to contact customer support and maybe it's not even possible. And then you have to wait for an update or maybe something is bugged. With programming you're so much more reliant on yourself and you can really just do whatever it is you want to do and you're not reliant on other people or on the tools that other people have built for you. But rather, you can just pretty much go and just do what you want to do without there being major roadblocks.

And then we'll also look at some essential packages in Python. In programming, you never want to reinvent the wheel. You always want to start off where the last person left off, and so the ability to program and be able to write simple programs you would need to teach yourself, but you wouldn't need to write highly complex mathematical packages or data analysis packages. Those are already out there. All you need to do is be able to download them and implement them in your code and they're going to work. They've been tested a lot, there's a huge community's working on them, on improving them and all of this is for the benefit of everyone. And so the whole community works together to improve it. No one's really directly trying to make a lot of money off of it, so they're not going to charge you all of these service fees and everything everyone's just trying to improve their package because if it improves everyone also benefits from it. And so we'll look at some of the libraries or we'll talk about some libraries that you can use especially in Python, to help you along your way with data analysis and to become a successful data scientist.

Chapter Two

Statistical Data Types

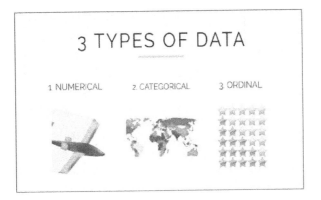

In this chapter, we're going to talk about statistical data types. We're going to look at the three different types of data which are summarized as numerical, categorical, and ordinal types of data. Now, these are the types of data that we talked about before, how you can't just expect your data to be numerical and so we'll see the numerical data but we'll also see the two other types of data that you may be encountering in your career as a data scientist.

Numerical Data

Numerical data is also known as quantitative data, and it's pretty much things that you can measure. Its great numerical stuff that you can do math with, you can compare it saying this Plus this makes sense A is greater than B these are all examples of numerical data.

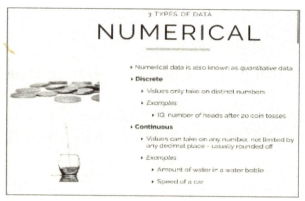

Numerical data can be split up into two

different segments. The first segment is discrete. Discrete means the values only take on distinct numbers and an example of this would be IQ or something like that. A measurement of IQ, or if you do a coin toss, the number of times that you toss heads, so you can have 15 heads, you can have 12 heads out of 20 coin tosses, you can have 500 heads out of a thousand coin tosses or 500 out of 600. All of these are distinct numbers. Now they don't have to be whole specifically, but they do have to be distinct. So that's the discrete part of numerical data then we have the continuous part.

In continuous numerical data, values can take just any number, they're not limited by decimal place. So a value can be 1.1 and then the next value would be 1.2, that's not continuous, that's still discrete because you have this step size of 0.1. Continuous means literally every number from start to finish can be taken on, and this doesn't mean that every possible number in the universe from negative infinity to plus infinity, and all imaginary numbers and everything that comes with it, that's not required for continuous. It could really be that just every number between 0 and 1 can be taken on. So for example, let's say you have a bottle of water, and this bottle of water can hold 1 liter. Now, if you fill your bottle up and it starts off empty and you fill it all the way up to the top, the amount of water you've had needed to take on every single number between

0 and 1 because you can't just fill up water in small increments of say, hey, I'm going to put in 0.2 liters every single time because the water doesn't just teleport from A to B. But when you're pouring in water, it's more like we see in the stream here and the water level rises and rises and rises, so the amount of water that we have in our cup needs to take on every value between 0 and 1, that's an example of continuous data form.

But you see that we can be limited to be between 0 and 1, we don't have to start at zero and go all the way up to infinity or something, but it's just that the range that we're looking at, every single number can be applied or every single number can happen. Another good example would be the speed of a car. If you start and you're standing still; you're standing at a stoplight and then you want to accelerate and the speed limit is say, 50 miles an hour. To get to 50 miles an hour from your starting position, your car has to take on every single speed in between, and of course you won't see that. On your speedometer it would say something like zero miles an hour one mile an hour, maybe you can go to like, its going 0.1, 0.2, 0.3 or something like that. So it may look discrete to you but that's not how your car is going. Your car doesn't say , oh I'm going to go in these step sizes of speed, it's going to accelerate and it is going to take on every value starting from zero, going up to 50 miles an hour.

When you're in this transition you're going to take on every single one of those speed values. That's how continuous data looks like.

It's important to understand the difference between discrete and continuous because you may want to approach it differently. Now of course, if we're dealing with computers, our computers can't deal with infinite numbers and we have to cut off the decimal places somewhere, and so usually, continuous data is going to be rounded off at some point. But it's still important for you to know that you're dealing with continuous data here rather than discrete so that you there can still be other stuff in between here. And all of these things, rather than having specific step sizes and all you see is just a bunch of lines at every step size. But you can expect that when you have continuous data that everything is just filled up, that everything can, and may even well be in between certain places. So that's the important thing to note between discrete and continuous.

Categorical Data

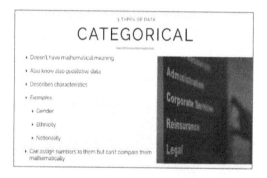

The next type of data that we have is categorical. Now categorical data doesn't really have a mathematical meaning, and you may also know it to be qualitative data. Categorical data describes characteristics. So a good example of this would be gender. Here, there is no real mathematical meaning to gender. Of course, if you have good data you can say male is zero and female is one, but you can't really compare the two numbers even though you assign numbers to them, and you may just do this so that you can split it up later or that your computer can understand. But it doesn't really make any sense to compare. You can't say is male equal female? You can say male is not equal to female but you can't really say is one greater than the other or is one approximately equal to the other. Those things don't really make sense because they're not well-defined and you can't really add them up either. You can't say male plus female. So you can't really apply maths to categories, but they are nice ways to split up or group your data and they provide these nice qualitative pieces of information that are still important. It is just you can't really go that well about, plotting them on a line or something like that.

So those are important things to note with categorical data. And then, another example would be ethnicity or you could also have nationality. All of these things are examples of categorical types of data. Like we said, you can assign numbers to them but that's really just for your code so that it's easy to kind of split them up but you still can't really compare them. How are you going to compare nationalities? There is really no definition for you know comparing one type of category to another.

Ordinal Data

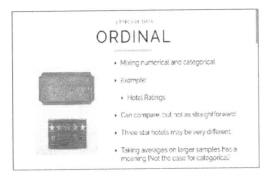

The third type of data that you can encounter is something called ordinal data. Now, ordinal data is a mixture of numerical and categorical data. A good example of this would be hotel ratings. So you have star ratings 0, 1, 2, 3, 4, or 5 stars or maybe even 6 stars or whatever it is whatever that hotels go by these days, but it's still not as straightforward to compare. I'm sure you've seen two different types of three-star hotels. One of them had the bare minimums, the beds were okay but it wasn't really anything special. And then you had this three-star hotels that you could have sworn were at least four-star. And so star ratings do make sense, we can say a four-star hotel is probably better than the three tier hotel because there have been standards, there are standards for these things they have been checked. If you go to a four-star hotel you know what to expect. But still it's not completely defined. So like coming back to this three star example it's very hard if you just say, hey, we're going to a three-star Hotel. It's very hard to know exactly what to expect because there are different parts of three-star hotels. There are three-star hotels that have developed onto like have a swimming pool and other critical amenities. And then there are those three-star hotels that are really more like hostels or something that just made it past the two stars place. So there it's much harder to define or to know what to expect now. If you take averages of these star systems though then you do get a much better idea of what's going on. So if you have consumer reviews or something like that and you say, Oh, from 500 reviews, our hotel has an average rating of like 3.8, then you know that the three star hotel that you're looking at is pretty much a four star hotel. It feels like a four star hotel even though it may not have all of those qualifying characteristics, that's the kind of feel you get from it.

Whereas from another three star hotel, you may have a rating of like 2.9 or something. This hotel is more towards the lower end of the three star. Some people may not even consider it to be three stars. And of course, you know this rating may be a little bit biased because they went to a different three hard star hotel first, and then they went to this one and they were expecting something completely else from the three star hotel. So they said this can't be three stars this is two stars but it's because of the way that the ranking system is defined and everything. And so when we have the averages of these ordinal numbers, then they start to make a little bit more sense

Exercise

So let's go over a small exercise and see if we can identify what type of data we're dealing with.

STATISTICAL DATA TYPES

EXERCISE

Classify the following data values to their data type:

▸ Survey response to happiness
  - Bad, neutral, good, excellent

▸ Height of a child

▸ Weight of an adult

▸ Number of coins in your wallet

So the first thing we'll look at is going to be the survey response to happiness. Now you have people filling out a survey and then one of the questions is, how would you rate your happiness? and it's going to be bad, neutral, good, or excellent. What type of data with this be? Well, this would be an ordinal type of data because it's still in a form of categories and you're asking for the subjective opinion. But it does make sense so you can still compare them you can say excellent is greater than good, good is greater than neutral; neutral is greater than bad. But what exactly does it mean to be good and excellent? You know where do different people draw the line for this? There's still a little bit of vagueness involved but generally it does make sense and you can compare it and if you have a lot of surveys and you averaged them, the values you're going to get are probably going to be very well representative, or at least pretty good representative.

So if we look at the next thing which is going to be the height of a child. What type of data is that? Now we can say it's probably numerical. And well it actually most definitely is numerical. So the height of a child is a numerical value. But let's go a little bit deeper and say, is the height of a child discrete or is the height of a child continuous? Well, even though when you measure height you get something like five foot, five foot three, or 160 centimeters or something like that. It's not a discrete value because to get that height, you have to have reached every single height before. And so even though at the moment, you may be measuring it you're kind of rounding it off to how much your measuring tape can measure. So your measuring tape is kind of limiting the height but if you had a super precise measuring instrument, you could measure not just five foot three or something like that, you could really go into detail. with the inches and the decimal places and there and everything kind of going on. So the height of a child would be a numerical data type but it would be continuous.

Now let's talk about the weight of an adult. Do you expect the weight of an adult to be either discrete or continuous? So we can probably agree that it's numerical because it's a weight value, it's pretty much defined to be a number and what do you expect it to be discrete or continuous? Well the right answer here is going to be continuous again, because to reach a certain weight, they would have had to have reached every single weight in between before. So again the weight is something that we can consider to be continuous.

Finally, let's look at the number of coins in your wallet. Again we can already by the name it says a number of coins so we can probably agree that this is a numerical type of data, but the number of coins in your wallet would that be discrete or continuous? Well the answer would be discrete because it doesn't really matter what's your note, your coins could be 50 cent pieces that could be 25 cent pieces ten or five or ones or anything you know like a two or something like that, but we can sum up your to a whole number so you can have one coin you can have two, you can have three, but you can't have infinite fractions of a coin you can't have say you know the square root of two number of coins that doesn't really make sense. So you have a defined step size, you have one coin, and then if you have a second coin, then you have two, if you have a third coin you have three. You're going in step sizes of one so for the number of coins in your wallet we'd be having discrete numerical data.

Chapter Three

Types of Averages

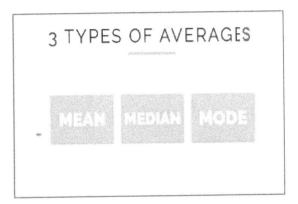

Now we're going to see the three different types of averages which is the mean, the median and the mode. Let's get started with the mean.

MEAN

- The typical "average"
- Sum of all your values dividend by the number of values
- Pros
  - Easy to understand
  - Takes into account all the data
- Cons
  - May not always be the best description
  - Affected by outliers

Now the mean is the typical average that you know and really what the mean is, is you just sum all of your values up and then you divide them by the total number of values that you have. Now the great pros of the mean is that it's very easy to understand. It makes sense, we just have everything we have and add it all up and then divided by what we have and that should give us a good representation of what is the average. And it also takes into account all of the data on them. So since we're adding everything up and then but dividing by how much data we have, we're taking into consideration every single data point. Now there are some problems with this. One of the problems is that the mean may not always be the best description and we'll see why when we look at examples for when we should use the median and the mode and the mean is also very heavily affected by outliers.

So since we're taking everything into consideration if we have big outliers that's really going to change how our mean looks like. So if we just have normal values between like 1 and 5 and all of a sudden, we have like 10,000 in there, that's really going to affect our mean. So mean is heavily influenced by outliers and the bigger the outlier, more the mean is influenced by it.

So let's see some examples of the mean we'll go through a worked example first.

EXAMPLE: MEAN

Data set: 22 22 23 24 25 25 26 26 26 27 39 59 79

Step 1: 22 + 22 + 23 + 24 + 25 + 25 + 26 + 26 + 26 + 27 + 39 + 59 + 79 = 423

Step 2: 423/13 = 32.54

Mean = 32.54

Useful for:

▸ The time it takes you to walk to the supermarket

▸ Exam score for a class

▸ Amount of chocolate required to satisfy a craving

We can see our data set here which is just a bunch of numbers and what we're going to do to calculate the mean is, we're just going to take every single one of these numbers and we're going to add them up and we can see the total result that we get here. And then the next thing we're going to do is, we're going to take this total result we're going to count the amount of data points that we have, and we're going to divide one by the other which then gives us our mean as we can see in the picture. So that's an example calculation of the mean. But let's see some example applications of the means. So when should we use it? Well, good application would say, if you look at the time it takes you to walk to the supermarket. Sometimes you walk a little bit faster and maybe it takes you 20 minutes to get there. sometimes you walk a little bit slower, it takes you 25, but on average it takes you somewhere like 22 or maybe 22 and a half minutes or something like that so if you say I'm going to go to the supermarket you're like it's going to take me this much time to get there.

Another good example of the mean would be exam score for a class. So to get a good understanding of how people do in an exam or in a class, you can look at the mean exam score last year. And since our exam scores are in a smaller range, a mean is going to be good to use it because you can get anything between 0 and 100. But realistically speaking, no one's probably going to get a zero. So your range is even smaller and so you're less affected by outliers and you kind of know how hard a class is going to be just by being able to compare their means. So if you look at one class and its mean is higher than the other, but they have a large number of students or something, then you can probably say, hey, it's easier to get a good grade here or something like that or maybe you know some of these simpler overviews without diving too deep into it.

Another good example of the mean would be to say how much chocolate do you require when you get this sweet craving? And you're not going to say, oh, I require one chocolate bar, two chocolate bars, or three bars. But likely you're going to say, on average you I require maybe three-quarters of a chocolate bar. Sometimes I may want a little bit more because I feel like it. And when I start eating chocolate I crave it even more. Sometimes, I have it at first and the taste doesn't sit right with me so

I have a little bit less. But these are kind of the amount of things. So if you have this craving you know either you say oh I'm going to try to be strong or you like hmm well I know this feeling and I know if I eat about you know three-quarters of a bar of chocolate or something, I'm going to feel good. My craving is going to be satisfied so you know what to expect. So these are some of the examples for how we would deal with a mean well when we would use mean.

Median

3 TYPES OF AVERAGES

MEDIAN

- The middle value in your data set
- If you have even number of data points, it's the mean of the middle two values
- Pros
  - Can sometimes be a more accurate description than the mean
  - Evenly splits your data
  - Doesn't care about outliers
- Cons
  - Doesn't give you much information on the rest of the data

So let's look at the next thing which is going to be the median. Now the median represents the middle value in your data set. Now if you have an even number of data points, you don't really have a middle value. And so in that case, the median is going to be the mean of the two values. So it's going to be the two median values added together and then divided by two. So the pros of using a median value is that the median can sometimes be more accurate than the mean and we'll see some examples of this. the median also evenly splits your data so you're not really affected by the mean in the sense that if you have an outlier in the mean, and it drags everything to the right, it could be that your outlier drags things so far to the right that all of your data is to the left of the mean and only the outliers to the right so that would be an extreme case, but that can happen.

Whereas the median is always located directly in the center of your data, and the median also doesn't care about outliers. So if you have huge outliers at the beginning and at the end, it doesn't really care because outliers by definition aren't very common because they're outliers. And so if you have them at the beginning or house them at the end, they're going to be very few in number which makes them outliers, therefore the median doesn't really care about outliers that much. A con though is that the median doesn't really give you much information on the rest of the data. Sure you know what's at the center but you don't know how everything around it behave, you only know where the center of our data is.

So let's see some examples we will do a working example first where we see our data set here and we can count how many values we have is we go from left to right then we can say we've got 1 2 3 4 5 6 7 8 9 10 11 12 and 13 data points so we've got an odd number. And so our median value, our center value is going to be the seventh data point because it's 6 from the beginning and it's also 6 from the end. It is equally spaced both from the beginning and from the end, and so that's why we see our median value here is 26. It's located directly in the center.

Now what is the median useful for? Well the median is often used if you look at household incomes for a country because if you were to use the moon then these billionaires they would just completely you know they would give you a false description of what really an average household income is because normally, if you have you know like an average value and you can say oh the average household income from this family would be say $40,000 or something like that or that would be the median value. But if you were to use the mean instead, then all of the billionaires and all the millionaires in the country would change that household income and then you would say, oh, you know the average household income per family would look like $60k and that's a bad representation, because that doesn't actually give you a realistic look at what the average household family has. And the average household family really does it's you know centered at $40k. And sure, there are people below and there few people above that threshold, but that's what's in the middle. Whereas if you were to use the mean instead for your average, you would kind of get this inflated household income which wouldn't be representative to the rest of your and the rest of the country.

Another good example of the median would be the distance that people cover to get to work. So if you look at this in terms of kilometres, some people walk to work, and its one kilometer at most. And then there are those who needs to travel for a short distance, most people travel around three kilometers to work. And sure, there are some that travel much further because they want to live outside of the city, and there are some that travel very short distances because they have a house right next to the office, or their house is the office, depending on where you are working. But then you can look at how do people travel to work? What time or what distance do they need to cover? That would be another good use of the median.

Another good median value is what do you usually spend when you buy a new item of clothing? You know sometimes you may go to that expensive clothing store and you could get a jacket that costs north of a couple hundred euros or dollars whatever system you want to use. And sometimes you can go to a second hand store and get it for very cheap. But usually if you go into stores, a jacket I don't know maybe cost you like a hundred dollars or something like that, and so you know if you go out you can expect to pay about $100 no not really you know taking that much accountant to what store you are going into. So most of the stores that you're going to visit are going to have that price for the jacket, so that would be another good use for the median.

Mode

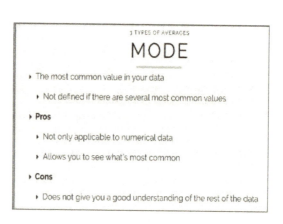

Let's   look at the third type of average that we can do, which is the mode. Now, the mode looks at the most common value in your data, and it's not really defined if there are several most common values, but if there's only one most occurring value, then that's what your mode would be. The advantage of using the mode is that it's not only applicable to numerical data. So if you look at categories for example, then you can say, hey, we've got five people from the US, two from Canada and one from France. And you know that the mode is going to be the US because there are five people from the US. So mode is the great average that's not only applicable to numerical data in this sense, but you can technically also apply it to categories or to ordinal numbers if you wanted. So that you can say the most common country that we have here the average country that we would expect here is the US. And sure, there are other countries but the average or the most common one is going to be the US in this case.

And then of course, and the other Pro is that we allow to see what's most common, what pops up the most. So that's a great use of the mode. If there are cases when recurring values happen a lot, which is the case for discrete numbers for example, in discrete numbers, values recur often and so it's good to use the mode. A disadvantage of the mode is that it doesn't really again give you good understanding the rest of the data, similar to what we had for the median. But also it's not really applicable if you just have a bunch of different types of data, then there isn't really going to be a mode if there's not enough of each data. It's not really good to use the mode you don't want to have thousands of data points and the most reoccurring value it reoccurs like three times that's not good. You want to use the mode for situations where data re occurs often so like we saw the country example.

But let's actually see a worked example but also some other examples for the mode.

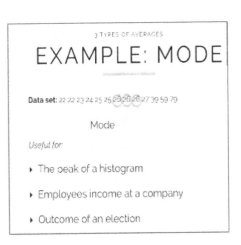

So a worked example here; again we take our data set and we can count how many times different numbers appear and so if we go through the numbers, we'll see that twenty six occurs the most and so that's going to be our mode here. So we've got 22 and 25 that both occurred twice, but 26 occurs three times and so 26 is going to be our mode since it is our most occurring value. Now the mode is going to be useful for things like the peak of a histogram. If you don't know what a histogram is don't worry, we'll cover that later in the book, when we go into data visualization. But the peak of a histogram that's going to show you the mode of the data, the most occurring data.

Another good use of the mode will be if you look at employee income at a company, because at a company, you can again have the boss which takes off the mean, and you can have higher level employees too, which we shift the median. But if one third of your employees earn minimum wage, that's going to be the best average, or say 40% of your employees earn minimum wage are probably not your employees because that wouldn't be a very good system to have. But a 40% of the employees at the company that you're looking at earning a minimum wage that's not a really good thing to have.

And if you look at the mode, you'll easily see that the average in this case would be to earn minimum wage because that's what most people earn. And sure, the boss or the CEO may shift the mean up heavily and then the fact that you have higher ups, if you look at the median value, you may even well be too far to the right that you really don't consider these employees that all are in the same amount. But you really want to get that description, which is what you get here from the mode.

And then also, the outcome of an election is where you use the mode for. And sure, sometimes you may only have two values, sometimes you may have three, but if you have different candidates and say you have five different candidates, then the person with the most votes is going to win the election because they have the most. And so there again, you'll use the mode.

Chapter Four

Spread of Data

In this chapter we're going to look at a spread of data. We're going to start off with looking at the terms range and domain, then we're going to move on to understanding what variance and standard deviation means and then finally, we'll look at covariance as well as correlation.

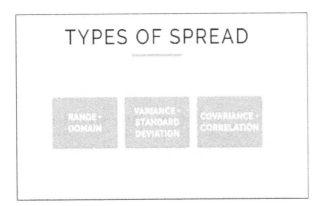

Range and Domain

Now let's start off with the range. The range is basically the difference between the maximum and the minimum value in our data set. So that's simple to think about. Let's just kind of go through this with a work example. Let's set up a company in the town, and this is the only company in the town and the owner of the company earns a salary of $200k a year, and then the employees, you know they all have different salaries but the lowest employees or maybe the part-time workers earn something like $50k a year. So we've got data ranging from $15k up to $200. And so our range is the difference between the maximum and the minimum value in our data.

RANGE + DOMAIN

- **Range:** The difference between the maximum and minimum value of your data
- **Domain:** The values that your data points can take on
- Example:
  - Income for a town
  - One big business, the owner earns 200k a year
  - Many employees that earn between 15k - 150k a year
  - Range of income for the town is 200k - 15k = 185k
  - Domain of income for the town is 15k up to 200k
    - Someone working in the town can have an income anywhere within that domain

So we take 200 K and we subtract 15 K from it and we've got a range of 185 K in salary, so that's how big our salary can change. So if we start at 15k, it can go all the way up to 200k so that's 185K range of salary that people in this company can have.

Domain

The domain is going to be the values that our data points can take on, or the region that our data points lie in. so if we look at this example again, our domain is going to start at 15 K and go up to 200K.

So what the domain defines is, it defines the starting and ending points, or it defines a section in our data and so in this case the domain would define we would start at 15k and it would end at 200 K and what the domain tells us is that everything or all salaries between 15k and 200k that they are possible. But within this domain or within this company, it's not possible to have salaries outside of this domain. So if our domain again is 15k to 200k, then we can't have a salary of 14k because that's outside of our domain, and we also can't have a salary of 205 K because again, that's outside of our domain. So pretty much all salaries within 15 to 200 K are possible, anything outside of the domain is not possible because that's no longer in our domain.

Variance and Standard Deviation

Let's move on and look at the variance and standard deviation. And we'll talk about the variance first.

Variance

Variance tells us how much our data differs from the mean value. It looks at each mean value and it looks at how different each value is from the mean value and then it gives us the variance. It does some calculation and we don't really need to know the formula it's more important right now just to understand the concept of variance. And so what variance really tells us is how much our data can fluctuate. So if we have a high variance that means a lot of our values differ greatly from the mean value and that will make our variance bigger. If we have a low variance that means a lot of our values are very close to the mean value and that will make our variance lower.

VARIANCE + STANDARD DEVIATION

‣ **Variance**: How much the values in your data differ from the mean value

‣ **Standard Deviation**: Square root of the variance

‣ Knowing the range your data is in gives you information on how closely group your data set is

‣ Example:

  ‣ Two different countries (A and B) have the same mean height of 165cm (5'4") for women

  ‣ A has a standard deviation of 5cm (~2")

  ‣ B has a standard deviation of 10cm (~4")

  ‣ In country A, most women will be around about the same height

  ‣ In country B you can expect the women you'll see to be of very different heights

Standard Deviation

The standard deviation is literally just the square root of the variance. If you understand one, then you also understand the other. And now we can combine this if we know the range of our data to get a better feel for our data. Let's use an example where we have two different countries, countries A and B, and they have the same mean height for women which in this case will say is 165 centimeters, or 5 feet 4, and we'll say that the range of heights for them could be identical. let's say the range is 30 centimeters or something you can go anywhere from say 150 all the way up to 80 or we can even increase that and say like anywhere from as low as 140 up to like 2 meters, but let's just keep the range for these same. And they both have the mean height.

Now if country a has a standard deviation of 5 centimeters, which is approximately 2 inches, and country B has a standard deviation of 10 centimeters, which is approximately 4 inches. Then what you can expect knowing these values is that if you go into country A, the people that you're going to see are going to be much more similar in height. So our standard deviation is lower, that means our values differ lower from the mean, and that means a lot of the women you're going to see are going to be very close to 165centimeters or 5 feet 4 plus minus 2 inches. So what you can expect when you go to this country is that a lot of the women are going to be about that height. Whereas if you go to country B, they have a much larger standard deviation and so you can't really expect everyone to be about5'4 because it fluctuates a lot more. If you go to that country you can expect to see a lot more women of different heights both taller and shorter than 5 feet 4.

That's how we can use the variants in the standard deviation or the standard deviation to give us a little bit more perspective on our data and allow us to infer some things about our data.

Covariance and Correlation

Covariance will or already has the name variance in it, but covariance is measured between two different variables and it pretty much measures if you have two variables. Let's say we've got me drinking coffee in the morning and my general tiredness. If I use these two values and get data point, this is how much coffee I drank in the morning, and this is how tired I feel this morning or something like that. What the covariance does is it looks at how much one of these values differs or changes when I change the other one. What does that mean? For example, if I drink more coffee, what the covariance would look at is how much does my tiredness change. So that's what you do with covariance. You see, you say, I change one, how much does that affect the other thing that I look at? And our correlation is very similar to covariance, so we normalize the covariance by dividing by the standard deviation of each variable. What that means is we get the covariance for my drinking coffee, versus feeling tired, and then we would just divide by the standard deviation of me drinking coffee and a standard deviation of me feeling tired. And so really, what we're doing with the correlation is we're just bringing it down to relative terms that would fit our data better. That's the abstract idea. The important thing to just keep in mind is that we're looking at one and we're seeing how much that changes, and we're seeing how much that change affects the other one.

COVARIANCE + CORRELATION

- **Covariance:** How much one value varies when the other varies
- **Correlation:** Covariance divided by the standard deviation of each variable
- *Types of Correlation:*
  - Correlation of 1 (positively correlated) when one goes up, the other goes with it
  - Correlation between 0 and 1: when one goes up, the other tends to go with it (more so close to 1, very much less so close to 0)
  - Correlation of 0: one variable changing has no effect on the other (at least not linear)
  - Correlation between 0 and -1: when one goes up, the other tends to go down (more so close to -1, very much less so close to 0)
  - Correlation of -1 (negatively correlated): when one goes down, the other goes up
- **Correlation does not imply causation!**

There are different types of correlation values that we can have and they can range anywhere between negative 1 and 1 or so their domain is between negative 1 and 1, a correlation of 1 means a perfect positive correlation. So that means when one variable goes up, the other goes up. So for my coffee example that would be if I have coffee in the morning, then I also feel happier. So the more coffee I have, the happier I feel. And of course, there's going to be a limit. But let's say I only drink up to two cups of coffee and I can drink anything in between. And the more I have, the happier I am about it. That would be a positive correlation.

The more I have of coffee, the more I have of happiness. And so they would go up together and then when we get closer to zero, the zero point is going to mean no correlation to us. So anything between zero and one is going to be a slightly positive correlation. It's not going to be a super strong and we'll actually see some examples on the next page. The closer you get to zero, the more it means no correlation. So an example for the zero case would be that it doesn't matter how much coffee I drink in the morning, it's not going to affect the weather. They're unrelated, one does not affect the other. I could drink one cup of coffee during a sunny day and one cup of coffee during the rainy day and it's not going to change the weather, it's not going to affect the weather so they're pretty much uncorrelated.

And then we can also go down into the negative range. The closer we get to negative one (-1) or if we reach exactly negative one, that correlation of negative one means a perfectly negative correlation. And here we can take our example of coffee versus tiredness. And so the more coffee I have the, less tired I'm going to be. So coffee goes up, and tiredness goes down. That's how we can understand this correlation and it comes from the covariance. So it was important to understand the covariance, we usually use the correlation because we divided by the standard deviation of each is much better fit to our data.

Now there is one thing that's very important to remember; and that's correlation does not imply causation. So just because two things are correlated, that does not mean that one causes the other. A good example of this would be if I live in a climate where it's usually cloudy in the morning and I know it to be sunny in the afternoon, but every morning when it's cloudy I drink coffee and then it becomes sunny in the afternoon. Even though they may be correlated, me drinking coffee and it becoming sunny. My drinking of coffee does not cause it to be sunny, that's just by chance. It's just because it happens every day and by chance there's this kind of correlation that appears but that does not mean that me drinking coffee results in the weather getting better.

A causation would be me drinking coffee and me feeling less tired, or me drinking coffee and me feeling happy about it because I like the taste. Those would be causations. So that's an important thing to keep in mind just because things are correlated does not mean that one causes the other.

Let's see these things on a graph and so here we have the examples again that we've talked about but we can kind of see how the data would look like for different types of correlations.

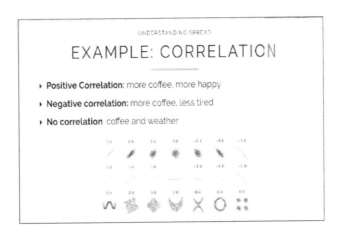

And so we can see a perfectly the perfect correlation of one. One goes up the other goes up. We can see on the left side and we pretty much get this really nice straight line. One value goes up, the other value goes up with it, and then the closer we reach zero, the less related or the less correlation there is between them. And then the more variance we have in data.

So we'll notice for the case of perfect correlation which is the one or the case of perfect anti-correlation, which is the minus one (-1), which again we had the example of more coffee, less tired. And in those cases we have a very nice thin line and our data doesn't jump around a lot, but the closer we get to zero the less we can see you know one causing the other, and the more we can see our spread out. So that's what correlation would look like in terms of graphics.

Chapter Five

Quantiles and Percentiles

In this chapter we're going to go through quantiles and percentiles so let's get started with quantiles.

Quantiles

What are quantiles? Quantiles allow us to split our data into certain regions that if we're dealing with probability, they all have the same probability of occurring. Or if we're just dealing with sizes of data, we want to split our data into equal regions. So that's what we can do with quantiles, just splitting everything up so that every time we split it, we have equal amounts of data. An example of a quantile would be something known as a quartile, and this is when we split our data into four equal regions, hence the name quartile.

So a quantile is the general name for doing this splitting procedure. And then if we say quartile, that means we're doing quantiles, but for four equal regions. And this is something that you'd probably often see on university admissions pages. And they say, the top 25 % of our applicants have at least a test score of 90%, and then they would say the bottom 25% of our applicants or our admission or admitted students have a test score of 70 % or 75 %, and then the median test score is 85 %.

So that's how you would go about quartiles. You would have the lower 25%, the middle 25 to 50 then you've got the 50 to 75, and then you've got the top 25 %; the 75% to 100. And so you've got these four equal regions which also include your minimum value at the very bottom, your maximum at the very top, and in the middle you've got your median values. So that's the value directly in the middle it's because you're splitting it up into four equal regions and so the value that separates the second quantile which would be the 25 to 50 from the third quartile which would be from 50 to 75 that value there would be the median value.

Percentiles

QUANTILES · PERCENTILES

PERCENTILES

- Splitting the data into 100 equal segments gives you the percentiles
- *Example:*
  - Getting a test score of 93% places you in the 99th percentile, meaning your score is higher than that of 99% of the people that took this test
  - This is also good for normalization, because it lets you judge someone's performance by having it relative to the performance of everyone else
  - A test score of 60% that puts you in the 95th percentile means the test was very difficult and you did much better than most other people on it

Percentiles may have been a name that you you've probably heard before. Percentiles again is an example of a quantile but instead of saying a quartile we do it for a percentile. I mean splitting it into 100 equal segments. You may have noticed percent means out of 100 or so, that's if you are familiar with percent and that's also the same kind of reasoning where this comes from and so we've got percentiles which means splitting into you 100 equal segments. An example of this is often used in test scores. If you've ever taken something like the SATs, you get a test score, but you also get a percentile. And the reason that is done is to judge, not you versus the test, but you versus everyone else. And so if it's a difficult test, then something like getting a test score of 60% but you're in the 95th percentile means your score is actually a lot better. And so what you can say with percentiles for example is that every percentile that you're in means you're better than that many other people.

For example, if you reach the 99th percentile that means you're better than 99% of the people that took the test. The 95th percentile would be 90 you're better than 95% of the people that take the test or something like that. And so that's why percentiles are often used for tests, and they're often used for normalization because they allow you to take into consideration. Factors such as: is it a difficult test? Is it an easier test? Or maybe more people are scoring higher. So they don't really judge you directly versus the test, but they normalize you against everyone else that took the test.

So you take the test, you get a score and then the percentile checks where that score lies relative to everyone else. And so these percentiles they allow you to give a good normalization and they allow you to do great comparisons, because they allow you to eliminate some of these factors of test difficulty.

And of course there can always be luck involved and stuff and that may not get filtered out on an individual basis. But if you do this for a lot of students, and that's also why it's done in these kind of big standardized tests, you get a percentile along with your score so that you understand if, maybe your score is lower but the test was really hard you can still see that you did really well because people found this test really hard and it was even harder for them than it was for you.

Chapter Six

Importance of Data Visualization

In this chapter we're going to talk about the importance of data visualization. First, we're going to look at the role that the computer plays for us and what role the computer is actually made for, then we're going to look at what role the human should play in terms of data science, then we're going to look at presenting data and finally we'll talk about interpreting data. So let's get started and talk about the role that the computer plays.

The Role of Computer

Computer is much faster at calculating than human because that's what it's made for. It's made for crunching numbers, it's made for doing fast calculations. If you think about how faster computers are, there in the gigahertz range, giga means billions. So they just do billions of things every second. And so they're really good for doing repetitive things because they can do them so fast, and then we can give them these logical tasks in terms of programming and we give them a structure and they just do it and they can do it over and over and over again.

They're not going to mess up. They can just repeat the same thing they won't get tired of it and they're really good and really fast at doing these things. That's the role that the computer should play for you. It should be a means to get these hard number crunching and all of these things done. So there's really no need for you to work out all this complicated math because your computer can do it much better and much faster than you, and it's also less prone to error if you code it correctly. So that's the only part where you come in and it's only going to mess up if you mess up. But generally, our computer does exactly what we tell it to do and it's really good and fast at it.

The Role of Human in Data Science

Now what role should a human play in terms of data science? Well, humans have naturally developed to identify patterns and we've done this first for survival, so that if we're walking around somewhere and we see a big predator hiding, we can identify that pattern of the predator and we can pick it out even though it's trying to camouflage itself. So humans by nature have become very good at identifying patterns. And you can also see this if you look at the clouds and you see things or you see animal shapes and the clouds or other things. So those patterns aren't actually there, but humans have become so good at identifying patterns we can see things in many places. So that's what humans are really good at, we're able to look at things and we're able to pick out patterns.

Now another thing that's really good for humans is we are very creative, and through their creativity we can also use memory and bring outside knowledge and we can also use a general understanding. So these are all things that computers can't do. Computers are a means of getting stuff to us, but once it's actually there, it's our job to use our pattern recognition abilities. And of course, you can train machine learning algorithms for specific patterns later on, or specific cases and make them really good at that. But generally if you don't know exactly what's going to come, then our or your first step as a data scientist would be to try to identify these patterns. Use your creativity, use your memory, bring in all of these different things. Use all of these different things that make you human and use all of that on the data. All of these things that a computer just doesn't have any access to.

Presenting Data

So using or considering all this, the best way to do all this would be in terms of data visualization. You can't just show spreadsheets with a bunch of numbers, that won't really help you because looking at numbers, it's really hard to pick out patterns. The best way to do it would just be to plot values and then if we have these visuals in front of us, then we can really identify patterns. We can see things go up and down and we can see them fluctuating and we can see them make very thin lines. We can just look at a graph and see things. And of course, we need a little bit of practice to understand what that graph is trying to tell us. But once we understand the graph and in general, then you know we can look at new graphs and we can just see things.

So we can start to see patterns and they may not always be true, but that doesn't mean we can't pick them out. And then that's later on, you would also do some testing, trying to see if those patterns are true, if they make sense. But generally, data visualization is very good for this because it allows you to invoke all of your human characteristics; the things that are really good that you know make us human.

The things that we talked about earlier, all the things the computer cannot do. And sometimes if you deal just with these numbers, data visualization is for you in one sense, so that you can see these things and try to pick them out.

But also if you're trying to show these things to other people., So maybe you have to do a presentation in a kind of summary then you want to make sure that your data visualizations are good because the people that are going to be looking at it are much less trained looking at data analysing data than you are. And so if you try to convey them a message and just show them a big spreadsheet with numbers and just point out like here, look these numbers, you know they pop up and they're going to be like "what are you talking about?" so that's why it's really important to have really good data visualization skills; one of them is to enable you to do your job, but the other part of it is to show it to other people and to help you convey information to them.

And of course we talked about statistical values. Statistical values are very important and they can give us a good idea about the data and what's going on inside the data, but visualizing data is just taking it to the next level and statistical values aren't enough. They can help us, they can support us, they can give us ideas, but if we really want to understand what's going on sometimes we just have to take a look at what's going on and of course they are it's also important to make sure you choose the right visualizations and everything because other times you know may just look extremely weird, but t this skill of being able to present data both for yourself as well as for other people is very important for a data scientists.

Data Interpretation

The next item we want to consider is data interpretation. We have touched on this in the last section already but really with data visualization, it just allows you to see this data and it allows you to apply some reasoning to the system. And so if you look at data, either you see something, which is great, that means you can try to test something, see if it's actually there. Or you don't see anything, and that also tells you something that you aren't really able to pick out a pattern, that there isn't anything obvious that's going on, there may be something underlying that's more complicated but obvious to the user it's not there. All of these things allow you to easily or much more easily analyse your data and prepare what you are going to do after that.

Data visualization really gives you a deep understanding of what's going on with your data, and then when we interpret this data and we look at these visualizations. Maybe you see dips and maybe you see some hills somewhere, we can try to understand all of this by bringing in our outside knowledge. So again, what the human is really good at. We can bring in the context of things, maybe people are going out to lunch here and so that's why activity decreases or maybe everyone is coming to work in the morning and so that's why activity increases compared to 6 a.m.

We can bring in all of this context, we can bring in all of this understanding to try to interpret the data, to try to better understand what's going on and then of course, we're going to see hopefully some trends or patterns. Of course like I said, these may not always be there. We are actually so good at pattern recognition that we can sometimes see patterns that aren't really there. A good example again of this would be just looking at the clouds in the sky and you can see animal patterns maybe but that's really not there, that's just our minds identifying all of these patterns.

And that's pretty much why data visualization is so important to a data scientist. It's because this whole human aspect is just key in data science, its key in data analytics to be able to understand what's in front of you, to be able to understand these outside knowledge, to be able to contextualize this creativity that's really key to a good data scientist. A computer can help you with all of this. The computer can help you do the number crunching, a computer can help you set up the visualizations and it can plot whatever you want for it. But ultimately, it's up to you to choose the right visualizations to do, to look at the data, to be able to communicate the visualization well. All of those things are up to you and so that's why the human is so important in data science.

Chapter Seven

One Variable Graphs

In this chapter, we're going to look at one variable graphs, we're actually going to see some of the types of graphs that we can do that we talked about in the last chapter where we just looked at the importance of data visualization. So now we're going to go into data visualization and look at the types of graph that you may want to use, or that you may want to choose from.

The graphs that we're going to look at in terms of one variable graphs are going to be histograms, bar plots, and pie charts.

Histograms

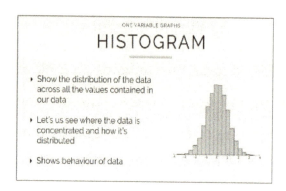

We can see an example of a histogram on the right. But what's really cool about histograms is that it shows us the distribution of the data, and it shows us the distribution across all the values in our data. It shows us what happens the least, and it also shows us what happens the most. Histograms allows us to see where our data is concentrated, and they also allows us to see how it is distributed. And through this, it shows a general behaviour. And so really what histogram is, it looks at each value and it just looks at how often the value has occurred. And so what we see here for example is that around o (zero), we have the most occurrence of whatever value we're looking at, and as we move to the left and as we move to the right these values start to drop off, so they start to become less frequent and that's what histogram shows us. They shows us frequency, how often these things occur. And there are different types of histograms that you can encounter. Generally, a histogram is just this plotting of frequency versus your value, and so there are different ways that this histogram can look like, one of them is the one that we've just seen which is a normal distribution or it's called

Gaussian like histogram because it follows this Gaussian distribution or this normal distribution that you know.

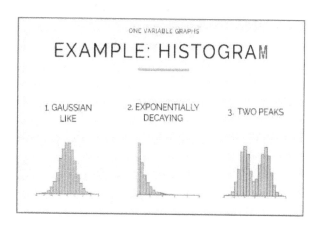

But we can also have like an exponentially decaying value, so we start off very high and the further we get away from that initial value, the quicker it's then going to decrease. You can actually compare that to the Gaussian like, or to the normal distribution. The normal distribution looks more of like a bell, it goes up and then curves down slowly, whereas the exponential cuts off very fast and then slows down later on. So they do have different behaviors. And then of course you know we can also get not just one peak like we see in this first case and the Gaussian like distribution, but we can also get things like two peaks, we can even get three peaks or more. We can have very large extended peaks. And so our histograms are means of showing us how this data is distributed. They are means of showing us what things occur most frequently, where our data is concentrated. But that doesn't mean that they're going to have a specific value and so they're of specific shape. There are many different shapes that our histograms can take on and depending on what shape that you get, that also tells us something very different about our data.

Bar Plots

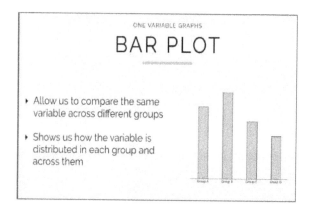

The next one variable plot that we'll look at is bar plots. And so bar plots may look a little bit similar to histograms at first, but they are very different in some sense because bar plots allow us to compare across different groups. And so that's what we see on the x-axis down there is we look at different groups and so we use the same variable but we can compare that variable over different groups.

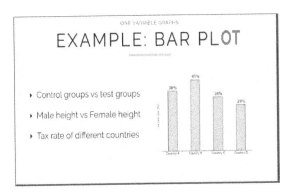

If we look at that in the example, what we see on the right here is we look at different countries and what we show is we show the average income tax. We see that country B for example, has the highest average income tax, whereas country D has the lowest income tax. So through this, we're still only looking at the income tax variable but we are able to compare it over different groups, over different categories if you will. So other examples would be if you look at control groups and test groups or if you're doing some medical study or maybe some psychology study or something like that. You always want to have your control group, and then you can have different types of test groups, and you can plot each of these groups as a bar plot. You can look at the same variable, but you can look how that changes over the different groups.

Another example would be something like comparing male versus female heights. So you've got one group that's male, the other group that's female, and you can just plot their average height. And then the tax, the income tax of different countries, which is what we seen on the right over here.

Pie Charts

The last one variable graph that we're going to look at is going to be pie charts. And what pie charts allowed us to do is that they allow us to section up our data and then we can split it into percentiles. And because of this, we can see what our data is made up of. So the whole pie corresponds to 100%. And then we cut it down at different slices and through that slicing and then hopefully also color coding like we've done here, and maybe even labeling or most definitely labelling so that you know what slice corresponds to what value we're able to see what categories our data is made up of.

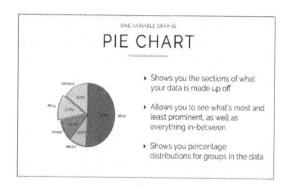

And so we can see what is most prominent, but we can also see what is least prominent. And again, here we can see also distributions, not as well as in the histogram, but we can still see distributions in terms of dominance, in terms of how many groups there are, is the data spread evenly? Is it heavily concentrated in one part of the pie? That's what we're able to do with pie charts we get this nice group overview of one variable. So examples of this would be you can look at ethnicity distribution in a university. And so you can have a pie chart, and just each slice of pie which is to represent a different ethnicity and depending on how much of our percentage they make up the total University profile, that's how big the slice of pie would be. And so you can see dominance of some ethnicities, as well as minorities. But you can also see just by how many slices that are, you can see how many different ethnicity groups there are.

ONE VARIABLE GRAPHS

EXAMPLE: PIE CHART

- Ethnicity Distribution in a university
- Star reviews for a product

And another example would be you can split up star reviews for a product. So rather than looking at the average star review, you can also just use a pie chart and you can see how many of my reviews are 5 stars, how many of them were 4 stars 3 2 and 1. And so there you can again also get this nice different overview of how the review system would work.

Chapter Eight

Two Variable Graphs

Now we're going to talk about two variable graphs, the graphs that we're going to look at are going to be scatter plots line graphs, 2d histograms or two-dimensional histograms, and box and whisker plots.

Scatter Plots

SCATTER PLOT

TWO VARIABLE GRAPHS

- Each data point is shown on the graph as a point
- Show you spread of data between two variables
- Allows you to see dense and sparse areas
- Can show correlations and trends that you don't get through simple numerical analysis

Now for a scatter plot, what we're doing is we're really scattering all of our data points onto a graph. And so pretty much every data point that we have, we put a little dot onto it on the graph. Scatter plots are great because they allow us to see spread of data between two variables. So we're always plotting one variable on the x-axis and another variable on the y-axis. And it just pretty much allows us to see how the data is distributed for these two variables. And then through that, we can also see more dense areas. We can also see some sparse areas, and we can also look at correlations.

So maybe you remember in the lecture we talked about correlations we were able to see through scatter plots where those correlations were, or where they weren't any correlation. So all of these things that's what scatter plots are really nice for. In scatter plots of course we can also use them to have like we see in the image little clusters. So not everything needs to be connected by a line or a curve. Maybe something is more like a circle. And so that's what scatter plots can show us too. They can show us these groupings and we see one cluster here, but maybe you have bigger plots, and then there would be smaller, like ten little different groupings for different things. So scatter plots are really great for that because they just show us where the data points are located for these two variables. And then we can see things ourselves like:

how do these look like? Does one variable affect the other? Is there may be certain groupings that we can see where are dense areas? Where it's sparse? Where are things concentrated? Is everything spread up all over the place? Is it very narrow and only in specific region? Scatter plots allow us to see all of these things very easily.

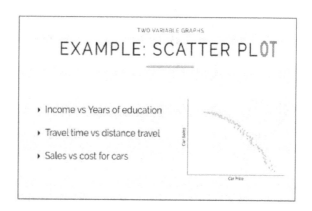

And so some examples where we could use scatter plots would be if we look at the graph on above, we can see something like a car price versus the number of cars sold. So each of these data points pretty much represents a car that's been sold and then the x-axis tells us the price that the car has been sold at and the y-axis tells us the number of cars that that have been sold at this price. And so what we see here, for example, very easily is that the more the car is priced, the less it gets sold. And then maybe you can think of that in terms of, well the more its priced, maybe people don't want to buy such an expensive car, maybe they found a cheaper version of it. So maybe it's just a branding thing, which is why it's more expensive. Maybe there's something just as good quality that's cheaper, maybe people just don't have enough money, that's probably a big factor too. That people just don't have enough money to buy these expensive cars and so that's why they drop off. And so it may look a little bit different in terms of profits, but the higher the car is priced, the less we see it being sold. So that's one example of a scatterplot

Then something else that we can look at is maybe the income versus years of education. So only we would look at on the x-axis, how many years someone has been educated and then we would look at their current income. And that would just be a point on the graph and we can do that for many different people. And then we can see how different education for different people how that affects their current income. That's another thing where we can do a scatter plot for. We can also go back to one of the earlier examples that we used very early on where we talked about people traveling to work and we can just plot the distance travelled versus the time it takes them travelled to work. And then we can see maybe some people travel faster. It could be that some people travel the same distance but one takes longer than the other because one goes by car, the other one goes by bike, and the other one takes public transport.

All of that we can see in these scatter plots and just take into account these different situations and see how that all looks for the more for the general population of our data or just generally for our data.

So scatter plots are really great as a first go-to just also identifying trends, identifying regions, and just giving a good overview of your data.

Line Plots

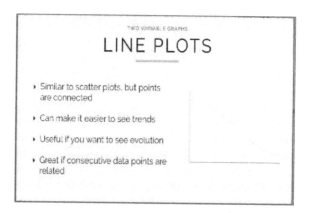

The next thing that we'll look at is line plots. Line plots in some sense are similar to scatter plots so we have the same bases of the X and the Y axis, but the points are connected. Now it's very important to know when to choose line plots and when to choose scatter plots

Line plots can carry a lot of advantages with them because this connectedness makes it very easy for us to see trends because we can see where these lines go. Not just trying to connect the points in our head, that's exactly what a line plot does is it connects the dots for us. We can see these lines, it's great if we want to see an evolution of something. So maybe we want to see an evolution over time, maybe you want to see an evolution over space, and evolution with people. Just if our data points are connected, it's great to use a line plot so if we know that whatever happened before is connected to what happens now, and it's great to use line plots because line plots show us how things evolve because they're all connected as a line. But if we're to do scatter plots and we just plot points randomly, if we go back to our car sold price example, just because someone bought an expensive car or if we look at the expensive car and it's been bought say like five times, and we look at a cheaper car and it's been bought a hundred times. There isn't really a logical connection to make between the two.

And so if we were to use line plots where we should use scatter plots, really what we'd see is just a bunch of lines all over the place, and so that's why it's important to know when to use line plots and when to use scatter plots because it can be very helpful. But if you use a scatter plot instead of a line plot, it's going to be a bit more confusing because you have to try to connect the dots yourself in your head. But if you use a line plot instead of a scatter plot, it's going to look really weird because there's just lines all over the place and you can't really see anything.

EXAMPLE: LINE PLOTS

TWO VARIABLE GRAPHS

- Distance vs. Time
- Profit versus number of employees
- Creativity vs stress

So an example where we could use line plots is when you have the typical distance versus time. So you can look at how far someone or what time it is and then you know how far someone has travelled.

Just a general curve of distance versus time. That's very common. And you can look at the profit of a company versus the number of employees. So the more employees they employ employee, how does that change their profits? So of course they have to pay the employees more, but maybe the employees can also do more work and hopefully that cancels out what you pay them and then increase this company profits. And then another thing we can see on the graph is creativity and how that changes with stress. So you can see that the more stressed out you are, the less creative you are. And here it's also good to use a line plot because you gradually advanced and stress. And so each point and stress is kind of related and the higher you go up in stress, the lower you go down in creativity.

And so there's this kind of relation, or we can see this evolution. So the more you get stressed out, the less creative you become. And so line plots are really nice here because there's not this chaotic movement everywhere, but it's very nice and it's very easy to see this line. It's very easy to follow.

2-Dimensional Histograms

The next graph that we want to talk about is 2-dimensional histograms. Now we've seen one-dimensional histograms in the last chapter where we looked at the spread of data, and we looked at the peaks and how you know things were distributed to the right and to the left but we can also do a 2-dimensional histogram. And somewhat, a 2-dimensional histogram is a one-dimensional histogram but it's a pretty much a histogram for every single point of the other variable that we're looking at. So really what these things allow us to see is they allow us to see the different distributions of the two variable relative to another.

.2-D HISTOGRAMS___ __

- Allows you to see distribution of two variables relative to each other

- Allows you to see where both variables clump, and how one falls of relative to the other at specific points

- Hard to see in scatter graphs because equal points will just sit on top of each other

So we can see here, for example, in the red region that for those specific values, they happen a lot. So that combination of values happens a lot. And so we're able to pinpoint these frequency occurrences again, and we're also able to look at drop-offs, but we're able to pinpoint that to two specific values now rather than just one, which is what we did to the 2-Dimensional histogram. These things are much harder to see in scatter plots because in scatter plots, if we have a value occurring a hundred times, it would just be the same dot and the dot wouldn't get bigger. Of course you can make the dot bigger yourself if you wanted to, or you could change the color. But really if you do a scatter plot and the same thing happens a hundred times it's just going to look like one dot. Whereas for two-dimensional histograms, we can see that it's not just happening once, but we can actually see the frequency of those variables or those two variables together.

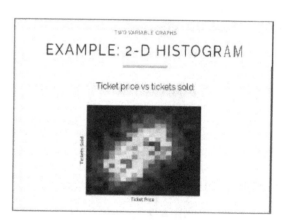

EXAMPLE: 2-D HISTOGRAM

Ticket price vs tickets sold

So an example of a two-dimensional histogram would be if we look at ticket prices versus tickets sold. If you look at the lower left corner we can see this red peak, so that's cheaper ticket prices, but the tickets are also sold often. So we know that tickets at that price are sold quite often. And these could be a new rising bands, these could be a standard bands that maybe you want to take someone on a date to but you don't want spend too much money on a ticket, but still a concert is a nice idea.

And so that's a good ticket price that sells a lot of tickets because it gives you the pleasure of the event without making it too expensive. And then if you move more towards higher ticket prices, and then if you move more towards more tickets sold, then you can see that for high ticket prices, which would be these big bands, then we can again see how many tickets we've sold. So we can see that for a higher price and if we go up and ticket sold. So if you want to see lots of tickets sold for a high price, then the red Peaks are going to give us all of these more famous artists. So that's one application. But of course, there are many better ones it's just these things you know if you're in the moment and you then you would realize, oh, this is when a two-dimensional histogram would be a great thing for me to use. So it is great know a lot of these graphs. And once you're in the moment, then it's much easier for you to pick out which would be best representative.

Box-and-Whisker plot

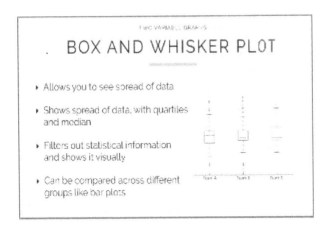

Finally, the last graph that we're going to look at is going to be a box-and-whisker plot. And what box and whisker plots allow us to do is they allow us to see the spread within our data. So it's not just like a bar plot which just shows us one value, but we can actually see the statistical spread. We can see median values which is what we see here, we can see quartiles the little dots on the outside actually show us outliers

And so what box and whisker plots allow us to do is they allow us to see the statistical information, but they allow us to see it visually. And that makes comparing across different groups, which is what we're doing here much easier. And a good example of that would be if we look at ticket prices for football games for different teams. So we have different teams and different teams of course use different stadiums and they have different popularities, and some teams may be much more expensive or the ticket prices may be much more expensive than other ones. We can compare these ticket prices using box and whisker plots, and then we can see what the higher end of these costs is. Those are going to be the more luxurious seats. And then we go to the bottom and those are going to be the less luxurious seats, probably the ones where you stand.

And then you have middle values, depending on you know the standard seats and where you are in the stadium. If you're close to the field, if you're further away from the field, but you're still sitting, all of these things we can see here and that's what gives us a spread. We can compare that across different teams and we can see the spread across difference teams, but we can also see which teams are more expensive, you know where do the prices vary the most for specific teams? And maybe some teams have a super launch and then they have your standing places that are just much cheaper. And so you would see a lot larger spread, or maybe some teams just have only seats and see you'd see a much lower spread. And so all of these things we are able to compare using box-and- whisker plots over different groups.

Chapter Nine

Three and Higher Variable Graphs

In this chapter, we're going to talk about 3 and higher variable graphs. So the graphs that we're going to look at are going to be heat maps, and then we'll also look at multi variable bar plots as well as how we can add more variables to some of the lower dimensional graphs that we've talked about earlier.

Heat Maps

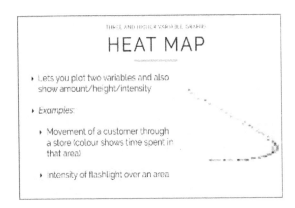

Heat maps allow us to plot two variables against each other. The x and the y, and they allows us show an intensity or a size or something like that in the Z direction or towards us. So an example of this which is what I've tried to illustrate in the diagram is a customer moving through a store. And we can track the path of the customer in the X and Y direction of the store so we can get this bird's eye view and see where they move to. And the darker spots actually tell us the positions where they spend more time at.

So we can see that they spend a little bit of time. At the beginning they moved in and then they stopped once, we see with dark spot being maybe they found the candy aisle or something. There was a specific piece of candy that they wanted and then they moved on, and then they started to go towards the corner a little bit, and maybe they reached the fruits and the vegetable section there and picked several things. And then they started to head towards the checkout counter, which happens at the very end and they were moving at a more constant pace. Sometimes they stop to look a little bit, but they just continued moving on. And so the three variables that we've shown here, we've shown their position in the store, and to their color. We've also shown the time that they spend at each position, so that's what we can use heat maps for.

And then another example of the heat map would be if you take a flashlight and you move it over the screen. And really what you're showing is the amount of time that you've shown the flashlight onto a specific region. So that's another example of the heat map. But usually, heat map as the name implies allows you to track positions. And so it's very often used for things like tracking customers through stores or just tracking general pattern, people location, where they like to spend their time. And the intensity that you see in terms of the color is usually the amount of time that they spent there.

Multi Variable Bar plots

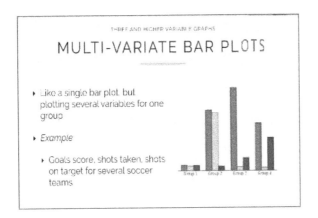

This is similar to a single bar plot where we just plotted one value over different groups. But rather than just plotting one, we cramped them together and we plot several. An example of this that we plot would be goal scored for teams, the shots taken on goal as well as the shots on target. And so we can see maybe there are teams that shoot less on goal or score less, but that's because they also shoot less and therefore they also shoot less on target. Or maybe there are some teams that do score a lot and that's because they shoot a bunch but they just don't hit the target that often or maybe there are really good teams that score a lot and they also shoot a lot on target. All of these things we are able to then compare over different groups. That's what we can use multi variable bar plots for.

If there are several variables that would give us a better understanding of the system than just looking at the variables one at a time, but it also be really cool if we could compare all of them then we could use multi variable bar plots for that and just plot them on the same bar plot and then we can see how they change within a group. We can also see how they change over different groups. We can also just add extra dimensions to lower dimensional graphs that we've had.

And so we're limited to three dimensions because that's the amount of space dimensions that we live in, but if we take a scatter plot for example, where we started off with just the X and the Y axis and points located, what we can do is we can actually add a third axis so we can take the X and the X and then we can add a Z and that gives us an extra depth dimension which is exactly what we see here.

LOWER DIMENSIONAL GRAPHS

- Add an extra variable to plots like line and scatter plots

- Same benefits as 2 dimensional plots but add an extra variable, allowing you to see extra relations

- Visualisation makes depth harder to see, since every snapshot is just 2 dimensional

So rather than just plotting on a two dimensional field, like a plane, we can actually plot it in a volume and so we can see this scattered ball that we've done. All that we've done here which is located at the center of our plot. And so this can be really cool because it allows us to see depth too. The problem with this is that we have snapshots every time and so really we're looking at two-dimensional snapshots. And so to get the best understanding of this, we need to rotate our scatter plots or our plots as we do them so that we can also add in our depth perception. Because right now for looking at it, it may look three-dimensional but really it's just a two-dimensional snapshot and to get the best understanding if our scatter plot is located more towards us and more towards the left. Or maybe it's just really high and close to us, or maybe it's really low and far away. To understand all of these things, we need to be able to rotate our scatter plots so that we can see it from different angles, which then gives us this depth perception.

And we can do the same thing with 3-dimensional line graphs. So here we see an example of maybe the position of a skier as they're skiing down a hill, and then we can kind of trace that through time and we see that they're going down the hill in this nice exact motion as you should and we can just track their position over time.

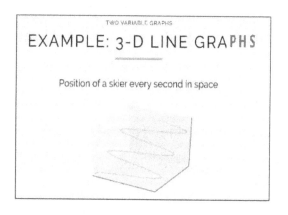

EXAMPLE: 3-D LINE GRAPHS

Position of a skier every second in space

So here we've added this extra dimension to the 3-dimesional line graph rather than just taking maybe a time and a position at a time, we've added a second positions or actually even a third position. So we've got the X to the one there's that position. And then we just trace it, and over time. And so that gives us this whole line here. And that's how we can take these lower dimensional plots that we've looked at before and we can just add extra dimensions to them if we want, as long as what we're looking at is still easy to see, as long as it makes sense, We're really just able to maybe just snap on another direction there and compare another variable.

Chapter Ten

Programming

In this chapter, we're going to touch on the third major section that is really great for data scientists or that should be an essential of data scientists, which is the ability to program. Why do we program? Well, there are different reasons why we want to be able to program.

The first one is going to be the ease of automation. The second one will be the ability to customize. And finally it's because there are many great external libraries for us to use that it would just make our job so much easier.

Ease of Automation

Let's talk about the ease of automation first. What do I mean by that? Well, being able to program really allows you to prototype really fast. It allows us to automate things and it also gives us the extra benefit if we have something in our mind, we can just take that and put it into the computer by programming it. And so we're able to automate everything very fast and we don't have to do these repetitive tasks, maybe copy pasting stuff into or from Excel or all these things. And if we just want to repeat something or we want to quickly change something up and just change a small thing, we don't have to do a lot of stuff. We can just change that in our code and then click play and let the computer take care of all of that for us rather than us having to do everything manually. So it's very easy for us to automate things and also for doing reports, it's very easy to automatically create these reports. All you have to do is set up your program to deal with the data that you're going to give it. And then it can automatically create reports every week. And the reports can be different because you give a different data and it should still look the same but the data values can be different and so that will just automatically create all these reports for you.

And you don't have to do that all yourself. The program does it for you, but you've built the program and you're giving it this different data. You're still doing all of the analysis. it's just you get to skip the part of copy pasting and like looking across and taking over the values and doing all the formatting of just doing the same report over and over and over again, all of that is taken care of for you. And all you have to do is just put in the right data, write out everything that you want to do and then click play, and let the computer handle all that for you because remember that's what the computer is doing and good at doing these repetitive tasks.

Ability to Customize

We also want to be able to program because it really allows us to customize. It's very easy once we go into data analysis and when we see things that we get these ideas that we want to expand or different directions that we want to progress our analysis into. And being able to program, it really just allows us to take all that and put it as a code and just choose that direction. And we can very easily dive much deeper into our analysis and discover things fast because it's up to us to where we want to go. And so this ability to customize with programming is very important because we're not reliant on anything else, we're not reliant on some software and maybe it breaks down or maybe we don't know how to perfectly use it. And we have to read the manual and read a Help section. And now we know how to program and we just type down exactly what we want to do, exactly where we want to take it, exactly what we want to see.

And we can customize very fast with that. We can also prototype very fast with that. And maybe if a visualization is not working, to turn a scatterplot into a line plot it's very easy. You just change one word. So all of these things are very easy to do with programming because we have all that power at our fingertips and we can just change everything that we're looking at, everything that's being calculated. Maybe we want to calculate an extra thing and take out something else because it's irrelevant. All of these things we are able to customize, and all of that we can do because we're able to program.

So really what we're doing is we're making the data ours, we're taking full control of the data we're taking full control of where we want to go with our analysis what we want to see and what we want to show.

So let's talk about first libraries, but also give you two great Python libraries that you should feel comfortable with or that you should consider using for data analysis.

So first of all what are libraries? Well, libraries are pieces of code that have been pre-written by others that you can just take in and use. A very good example of this is something known as a math library. And so that has all the square root functions taking to the power, taking the exponential, the sine the cosine, all of these things that you know and you want to use but you don't want to program yourself. So it pretty much avoids that middle step of you having to program the equation to calculate a sine because all of these things those are things that we don't want to do.

We don't want to get distracted from our target. We want to be able to do exactly what we want to do without having to program completely other stuff. And so that's what libraries are great for. They are developed by the community for everyone to use. You know everyone is helping each other, and these libraries they just bring a lot of power with it. And so one of these libraries is called pandas, and pandas is pretty much like Excel, but it allows us to do or we can do programming with it, which just makes it so much better because we can do things so fast with it. We can do all this customization, we can do all this automation, whereas if you give Excel too much stuff, too much to run, it would just start to crash because it has to handle all of this other things. All these other visual things, the UI and it's not a structure as well.

Whereas in programming your computer just goes through everything step-by-step. It doesn't have to take care of all of these visualization things. It just does the calculations down below. But we can still do all sorts of data management with them so we can shift our data around, we can drop columns, we can split things up, we can split things up by row, we can pick out certain rows, we can even do statistical calculations on our data so we can say, hey, calculate the mean for this.

We don't even have to make our own formula for calculating the mean, or for calculating the standard deviation or for calculating correlation between different columns. All of that can be done with pandas with just a couple of keywords. And so it's really easy to do data analysis with it because all of the functions that are there and we know exactly what we want to do, but we don't have to write the code for all of it. So if you wanted to look at correlations, we just say, hey, pandas do correlations. Rather than having to code all the correlations for ourselves and coding that whole algorithm. And that makes it really easy and really fast to get results and to get to where you're heading because you don't have to go into any of these middle places. You can pretty much just skip the middleman of having to write all of those algorithm yourself and you can just use them so that you have your start, you have your idea, you know exactly what you want to do and you can do exactly that to get to your goal.

The other library that is very cool would be Matplotlib which is what I use a lot for data visualization. It allows me to create graphs, allows me to visualize my data allows a bunch of customization so I can really just move everything around in it. I can move my spines, I can turn things on and off, all of these things are very easy to do with Matplotlib. There's a lot of great customization that I'm able to do with it. So these are two basic Python libraries that you should probably get to know or you can look at some of my other courses. One of them pandas would deal with the data analysis part and MATLAB would help you deal with the data visualization part of it.

So that's it, that's a super basic breakdown of the three main components of the otherwise vague term data science. If any of this has pick your interest, then you may have a data science future ahead of you and I encourage you to continue to pursue your interest.